Made In

第十勢 順鸞粉掌

右拳壓掌、向右
上方一揭、右腳
一蹬、左足向前
一步、身隨右轉
、左腳前伸、右
膝盤諸、成騎龍
勢、同對右手向
後一捋、左手向
下方發一切掌
、遇對左足是夫

第二十二勢 旱鳳朝陽

右手向外上揚
、再由懷內畫
蓀向上、左手
向右方蘊下、肘
落於腿前、右手
角微彎、右手
上舉、腑臂緻
屈、同對左足
跌回、足夫點
地、

CHINA

By Reed Darmon
with assistance from Kalim Winata

CHRONICLE BOOKS
SAN FRANCISCO

Page 256 constitutes a continuation
of the copyright page.

Library of Congress Cataloging-in-
Publication Data available.

ISBN: 0-8118-4202-9

Manufactured in China

Designed by Reed Darmon

Distributed in Canada
by Raincoast Books
9050 Shaughnessy Street
Vancouver, British Columbia V6P 6E5

10 9 8 7 6 5 4 3

Chronicle Books LLC
85 Second Street
San Francisco, California 94105

www.chroniclebooks.com

This book
is dedicated to
Wong Kwok Ying,
fellow traveler.

Introduction

Calendars, cigarette packs, labels for socks — the Chinese make so many everyday items with such care and charming design that it's impossible to throw them away. As you walk through the streets, markets, and shops, China's particular pleasure in craftsman-ship manifests itself everywhere you look. It's an ancient tradition, one that has survived for thousands of years.

The Chinese marketplace is ideal for taking in a visual feast of color and design. How can so many matchbox covers exhibit such painstaking artistry? Why is so much creative energy expended on fabric labels, tea packages, and store wrapping? The answer lies both in this age-old tradition of fine craftwork and in the Chinese love of collecting.

For example, hundreds of cigarettes brands, originating from remote towns of the west to the giant cities of the east, each sport distinctively designed logos, and at one time came with collectible cards in every pack. Full sets of these little treasures can be found today in flea markets and shops. You'll also see countless brands of tonics, ointments, and medicines that seem to have no limit to their beneficial qualities or the extravagance of their packaging.

And surely no country can claim a more prolific tradition of poster art. In the early twentieth century hand-colored block prints were turned out in huge numbers and pasted on front doors to bring good fortune in the New Year. Building on this custom, more sophisticated printing technology deluged public spaces with promotional posters and calendars bearing fantasy images of legendary China and Shanghai pin-up girls. After the Communist Revolution of 1949, poster production grew even more intensive, but focused on nationhood: fantasies of progress, agricultural abundance, and the space age.

Mid-century portrayals of the beneficent Chairman Mao clearly take their cue from the old posters of ancient deities — both appeal for blessings from a higher power. Today, posters remain in constant production, colorful, ephemeral, and so useful for enlivening a plain wall.

When commercial design arrived from the West in the early 1900s, China's beautiful, ancient writing system readily adapted to the field. Calligraphy traditional to classical hanging scrolls morphed into modernist logos with ease. The complex play of meanings in customary phrases transferred seamlessly from poetry to ad copy, often producing clever double entendres. A picture of a bat, wings outspread, on a label evokes in the consumer's mind long life and wealth, because the Chinese word for *bat* sounds like the word for *good fortune*.

Unique cultural themes run throughout Chinese graphic arts. Babies are shamelessly adored, represented like little gods. Radiant young women are everywhere, ranging from toothpaste-touting ingenues to gun-toting Red Guard heroines. Carts, pedicabs, and the swish of thousands of bicycles convey the pace of the streets in images of city life. Other popular motifs come from traditional stories like the Ming Dynasty epic *Journey to the West,* with its endless array of superheroes and odd-looking demons, and courtly tales like *Dream of the Red Chamber,* rich in imagery of love and tragedy. But in China, as everywhere, global homogeneity has made its inroads, replacing time-honored motifs with pop icons recognized anywhere in the world.

Made in China makes no attempt to be definitive in any area of Chinese commercial art. That project would take a library of books. Rather, it is a nostalgic and distinctly Western appreciation of China's artistry and productivity. Where I can, I've included information on how and when the item was made. For deeper investigation, this volume defers to the many Chinese designers, decorators, and collectors now exploring the last century of Chinese graphic arts with such intriguing results.

And because graphic art inevitably radiates from the cities, this collection tends to represent an urban life shared even now by only a minority of the Chinese. The metropolis, too, has a greater concentration of nooks and crannies in which cherished items are stored. As more and more old neighborhoods are torn down in China's great cities, the crumbling houses give up their treasures of preserved design like a last bequest. Appropriately enough, in the land that invented paper, it is images on paper that endure.

— *Reed Darmon*

These woodblock prints were made in a traditional style called *nianhua* and used for decorating the home during the New Year's holiday.

ABOVE: This door poster declares that having a boy in the house is auspicious, and when he plays music wealth comes in the door.

RIGHT: "The King of the Mountain," Weifang, Shandong Province.

ABOVE: **"The Joy of Fishing."** The lower cartouche states that this print was made in Nanxiao and that the design dates from the fourteenth year of the Ming Dynasty.

LEFT: A good luck poster for the
New Year depicting Ts'ai Shen,
the God of Wealth, with gold
falling from the sky (1950s).

四 時 報 喜

ABOVE: "Good News for All Seasons," a recent
block print celebrating abundance. The style and
imagery date back over two hundred years.

15

**These beauties grace
turn-of-the-century cigarette posters.**

LEFT: This domestic scene, painted by Mei Sheng, was one of hundreds of stock images made available by printing houses for use on advertising posters and calendars. Here it advertises cigarettes from the Qing Tao Tobacco Company.

ABOVE: A flyer for Creme de Lait facial cream.

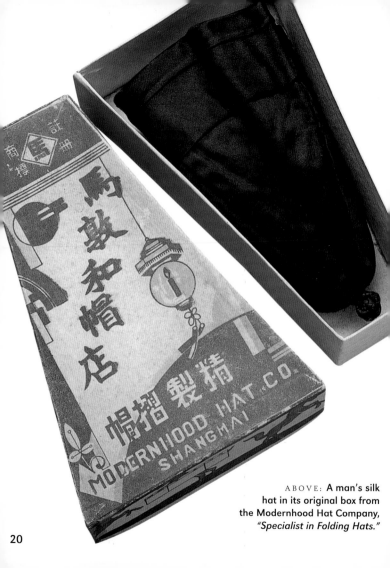

商標　註冊

馬　馬敦和帽店

精製摺帽

MODERNHOOD HAT CO.

SHANGHAI

ABOVE: **A man's silk hat in its original box from the Modernhood Hat Company,** *"Specialist in Folding Hats."*

ABOVE: "Modern Style," Good Luck
Coin brand satin hat, Beijing.

Tea boxes from
Hong Kong.

"View of Shanghai" (1930s). This poster, painted by Guo Chan, depicts Suchow Creek

圖景風海上

and the imposing Shanghai Mansion Hotel, center, which is still in operation.   25

26

ABOVE AND LEFT: These cards are for a popular gambling game similar to mahjong. The ones at left are printed and the ones above are hand-painted.

BELOW: Retirees enjoy a game of cards on the sidewalk.

ABOVE: Tiny hand-colored cards for "paper poker."

RIGHT: A royal flush is the winning hand on this "Five Color Calendar" printed by Chang Chuen Picture Company, South Fujian Province.

ABOVE: **A paper board game called "The Eight Immortals" by Yuen Kwan Foods and Toys, Kowloon.**

LEFT: **A paper soccer game with wooden dice, from Hong Kong.**

BELOW: Before the Revolution, tobacco companies included collectible cards in cigarette packs, which featured exceptional printing and design.

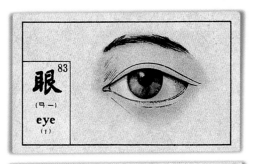

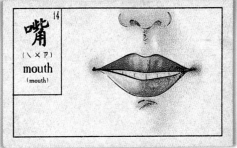

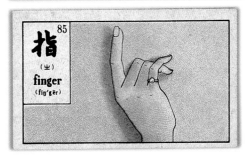

ABOVE: Three cigarette cards from a set showing English vocabulary in Chinese, phonetic Chinese, English, and phonetic English.

29

燈會第二十九圖　蝦蟆燈

16

燈會第十六圖　飛機燈

22

燈會第二十二圖　猢猻燈

18

燈會第十八圖　蟹燈

　　　Cigarette cards showing extraordinary lantern

creations for the annual spring Lantern Festival.

ABOVE: "Road Safety Tips," collectible cigarette cards from the Hwo Cheng Tobacco Co.

理髮

裝電燈

賣青菜

串籐椅

ABOVE: Collectible cigarette cards
featuring professions of the day.

紅孩妖

Images from the popular epic Journey to the West, written by Wu Cheng Yan in the Ming Dynasty, late sixteenth century.

ABOVE: The Red Boy, a demon dressed like a child, on a collectible cigarette card.

RIGHT: The future Monkey King appeals to the gods in an ad for Pirate Cigarettes.

西遊記　第一圖

重根育學源流出

"A Thousand Birds to Summon the Phoenix" is the title of this cigarette poster depicting auspicious birds gathering as an emperor's daughter plays music with her lover.

This unusual poster advertising Legation Cigarettes shows the scholar Zhang Quang lovingly darkening his new bride's eyebrows.

"Baochai Catching Butterflies," painted by Hong Zhiying (1940s). This poster depicts the noble and beautiful princess in the Qing Dynasty novel *The Dream of the Red Chamber*.

ABOVE: **Matchbox label with the legend "Long Live the People's Republic of China."**

RIGHT:
Matchbook
labels
featuring
colorful
animals.

THIS PAGE:
Vibrantly illustrated matchbox
covers show dancing,
badminton playing, and
fanciful transportation.

RIGHT: The text reads *"Manufactured
using Russian know-how"* in this advertisement for Wu Fu City Match Factory.

48

公私合营
蕪湖市火柴厂出品
安全火柴

据苏联先进经验配製

新产品
美化包装

改进技术
提高质量

中国百货公司蕪湖供应站包销

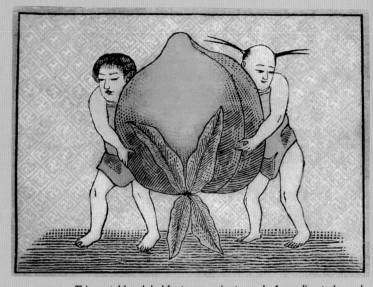

ABOVE: This matchbox label features a giant peach. According to legend, the God of Longevity will emerge from this fruit of immortality.

RIGHT: Chinese immigrants
brought their fine-printing
skills to several other
countries, printing matchbox
covers from India to Japan.

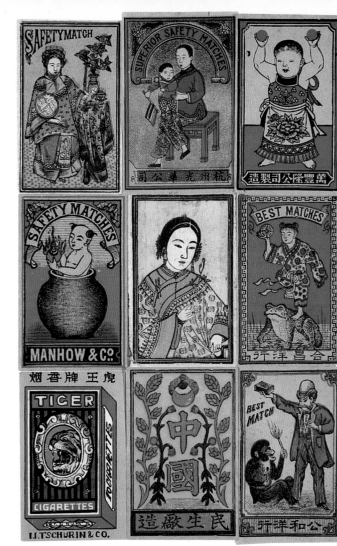

51

Pulp fiction from Shanghai (1930s).

The Vain Heroine   *The Red Scarf Gang*

Mystery of the Old House

The Mysterious and Beautiful Spy Girl

亂世風波

馮玉奇著　下集

香艷社會言情小說

紮腳三少奶

ABOVE: Shoes are the subject of interest in the novel *The Third Madame with Bound Feet.*

LEFT: *Love in Wartime*, a novel by Feng Yuqi, Qianjin Book Co.

ABOVE: An advertisement for "Cloudy" dresses reading *"China's first woman's dresses...new fashions, most experienced, best qualified."*

RIGHT: An advertisement
for Scenery Art Studio
offering art photography,
developing, and enlarging.

ABOVE: An invitation to
the tenth anniversary
celebration of the
"totally modernized"
Guangzhou Restaurant.

BELOW: An ad
for cigarettes:
*"The more you smoke,
the more you like it."*

ABOVE: Clockwise from top left:
"Double Girl Brand Powder," "Hygiene
Tooth Powder," "Tai Chung Wah Florida Water," "Beehive
Brand Wool Yarn," and "Kiss and Company Rouge."

58

LEFT: A label on a box of "Triple Fresh" brand noodles from the Hung Cheng Shing Biscuit and Noodle Company, makers of *"Machine-Made Quality Hanging Noodles."*

59

LEFT: **Blanket labels.**   ABOVE: **Sock labels.**   61

RIGHT: Label on
a bolt of fabric:
*"Manufactured
by Shanghai Qin
Gong Dyeing and
Knitting Mill."*

ABOVE: Fabric label that reads *"Superb Productions Sweeps the Country."*

ABOVE: **A fabric label depicting a famous supernatural battle at Lin Tong Guan gate, on the Great Wall at Shanzi.**

ABOVE: A package of cigarettes magically issues from the breath of an imaginary deerlike unicorn on a flyer for Ky Lin Cigarettes. Characters read *"Regain your power, promote Chinese products."*

BELOW: **Items for grooming, including a Tin Kwong "Super Quality" toothbrush, razor blades, a comb, and a bottle of cologne.**

RIGHT: **A wrapper from Daughter brand "Superior Soap."**

"Everyone must have Everyone Balm," states this a poster by the Earth Brand Cosmetics Company.

無敵牌

大滿

霜 蝶
BUTTERFLY CREAM

ABOVE: **"Morning Frost Butterfly Cream."** The packaging reads *"Protects from the ravages of sun, wind, and age."*

ABOVE AND RIGHT: Boxes of sweet
dried lichees exported from Canton.

LEFT: **Box from the Laou Kiu Woo Silk Company store, Nanking Road, Shanghai (1930s).**

BELOW: **Nanking Road today.**

LEFT: **Box for a garment made of "Moon Goddess Silk," from Sheung Ou Fabric Store, Hong Kong.**

ABOVE: Cabinet card from the photography studio
Pow Kee and Company.

A B O V E: **Photos from Swan Studio featuring stylish settings.**

LEFT: Hand-painted studio photo of a young woman in a heroic pose. Above the gate on the backdrop are the words *"Rejuvenated World."*

ABOVE: "Happiness" box camera,
Tianjin Camera Products Company.

ABOVE: **Five-goats camera from Guangzhou Camera Factory (1970).**

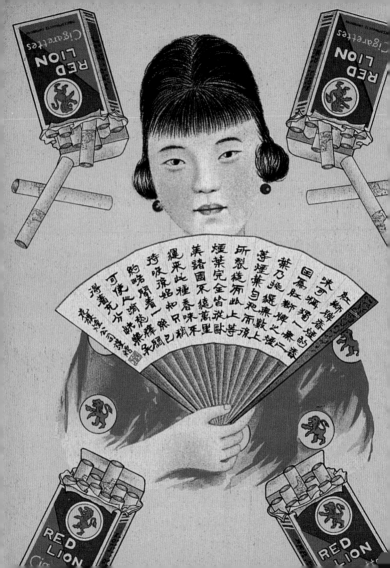

ABOVE: Small ten-cigarette packs from the 1930s.

LEFT: The characters on the fan read *"Red Lion Cigarettes . . . It gives smokers a love of its flavor, and the pleasure of forgetting any sadness and grief."*

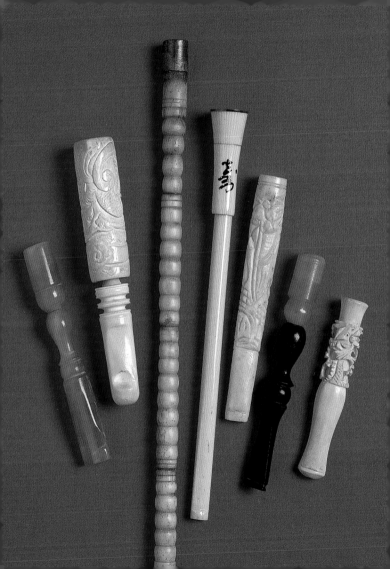

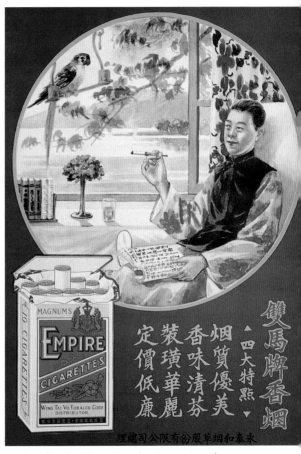

經濟時間 避免麻煩

ABOVE: The text on the counter reads *"To save time and to avoid trouble"* on this flyer for China Travel Bureau, Shanghai Headquarters (1930s).

ABOVE: "Holiday Medicine Box," by the China Medicine Manufacturing Company, contains pills for travel sickness.

ABOVE: **Clay traffic whistle shaped like a woman police officer.**

ABOVE: **Calendar girl painted by Huong Zhi Ying (1930s).**

LEFT: **"Wind Resistance Matches," Teng Ta Match Factory.**

RIGHT: **The "Forever" bicycle.**

ABOVE: **The image of refinement on a flyer for Umbrella Brand Cigarettes (1930s).**

LEFT: *Cheongsams* ("long dress"), a revolution in female self-expression, including a pattern in "burnt" silk from the 1930s (bottom).

ABOVE: This label for Tian Yi Silk Fabric and Dye Company reads "Social Flowers," a euphemism for women who dance for money.

LEFT: Blue glaze teapot.

LOWER LEFT AND UPPER RIGHT: "Cloudy White," chromed copper teapots, by Wang Da Yoo silversmiths, Zhe Jiang Province.

BELOW: A modernist earthenware teapot.

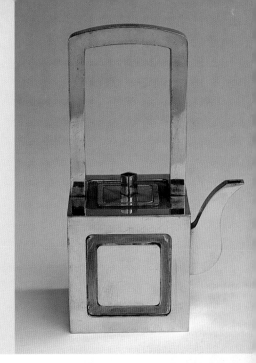

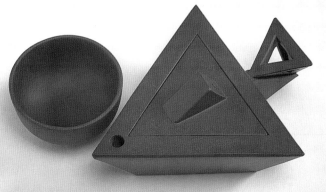

LEFT: Tissue label for a crate of wholesale tea from Taiwan (1940s).

ABOVE: Afternoon tea in the famous teahouse at Yu Yuan Gardens, Shanghai.

大華鐵廠

上海南京路

ABOVE: Ad for Diaward Steel Furniture Company, Limited: *"For those who desire modern charm in chrome-plated metal furniture."*

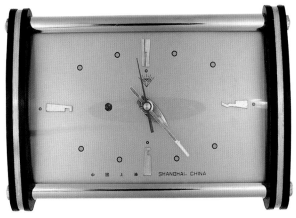

ABOVE: **Clocks from the Diamond Clock Company, Shanghai.**

103

良友

第一百十七期
四月號

THE MODERN MISCELLANY
No. 117 April 193
海時圖書公司印行
40¢ 每冊四角

ABOVE: The cover of *The Modern Miscellany*,
a pictorial magazine, April 1937.

LEFT: The cover of *Young Companion*,
a pictorial magazine, May 1937.

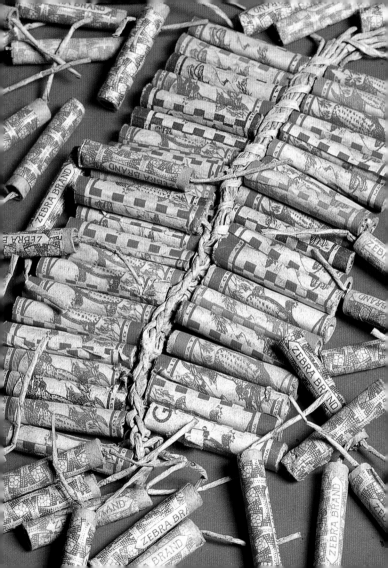

LEFT AND ABOVE: **Class C (medium power)** firecrackers imported to roadside stands in the United States, from the 1960s.

ABOVE: **Package of Jungle Brand Extra Selected Flashlight firecrackers (1940s).**

RIGHT: **The warning *"Do not hold in hand after lighting"* seems to be ignored in this detail from a label of Children Brand Fireworks, manufactured by Mr. Tang Bick Tong, Macao.**

Firecracker labels from the 1940s, 1950s, and 1960s.

LEFT: "Five-Color, Thunder, and Spitting Pearls," firecrackers by the Yick Loong Company, Macao.

Popular brands of firecrackers exported to the United States (1950s–1960s).

ABOVE: **A generous selection of candies at
the entrance to a food market, Beijing.**

"Acrobats Coliseum Show" poster by Chang Yi Ching, Shanghai People's Publishing Company (1959).

ABOVE AND BELOW:
Postcards of acrobatic
feats published by the
Shanghai People's
Publishing Company.

RIGHT: *"The Art of
Acrobatics, including
a person shot from
a cannon,"* reads a
poster for the Tsang
Guo Liang Magic
Troop Premiere Show.

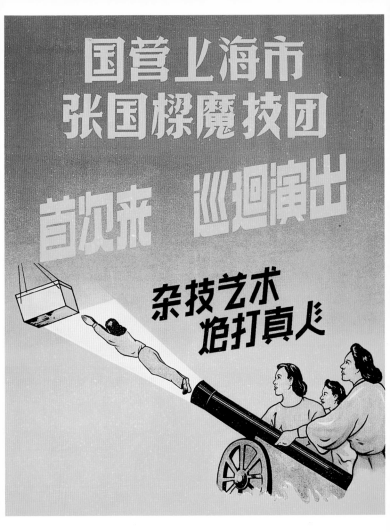

国营上海市
张国樑魔技团

首次来　　巡迴演出

杂技艺术
炮打真火

A poster for the legendary Shanghai Da Shi Jie amusement center, titled "Art and Literature Are for Laborers, Farmers, and Soldiers" (1965).

EFT: Calendar girl (1940s). ABOVE: Post-Revolution farm girl (1962).

"A Healthy Beauty,"
Da Hwa Offset Press (1930s).

wers of the Four Seasons," painted by Yang Fu Rue, First China Printing Co. (1955).

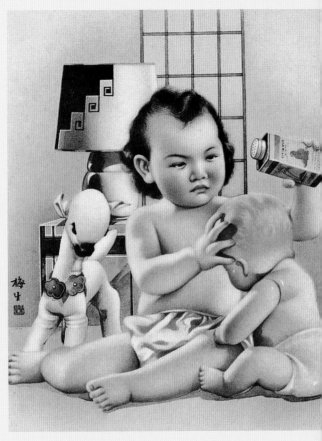

ABOVE: A poster painted by Mai Sheng, a prolific illustrator of domestic scenes (1950s).

LEFT: A New Year's poster titled "Good Harvest, Year after Year," Jilin People's Printing Co., Changchun (1960s).

童樂牌

BABY

ABOVE: Clockwise from top right: "Fat Baby Brand Fruits and Candy," "Chubby Children Worm-Killer Medicine," "Five Happiness Chubby Child Baby Powder," "Zebra Brand Little Angel Powder," and "Wang Heng Brand Medicine."

LEFT: "Happy Baby," a generic label from the 1960s.

LEFT: A generic advertising image painted by Zhi Guang (1940s).

THIS PAGE: Affordable toys for boys and girls.

133

RIGHT: Babies visit the
moon goddess in a
New Year's poster.

ABOVE: A noise-making toy called "Crying Tiger."

ABOVE: The Universe Car,
with "mystery action."

LEFT: "Little Visitor in Space,"
a New Year's poster from 1980.

ABOVE: This metal toy features sound, lights, and movement.

RIGHT: This poem was printed on the original
poster "Dream of all Children," by the
Shanghai People's Art Publishing House:
"Stars shine brilliantly bright,
clearly seen in a telescope by the eye.
When our modern science succeeds,
we materialize travel to the universe by flight."

ABOVE: Water, sparks, light, and noise: toy pistols for export.

BELOW: **The Pudong district of Shanghai — China's vision of the urban future.**

ABOVE: *"Dream vehicle for long-distance travel."*

ABOVE: A curious procession of "High-Ranking Senior Officials" on a sheet of collectible cards.

ABOVE: Ornate children's clothes to be worn
on festival days or at family parties.

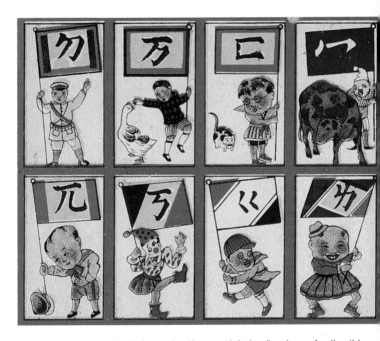

ABOVE: "Let's learn the Chinese Alphabet," a sheet of collectible cards designed to help pronounce Chinese characters.

LEFT: Coin bank.

ABOVE: Students from Yun Chang School on a field trip to Shanghai.

RIGHT: A selection of children's primary-school books from Shanghai and Hong Kong.

ABOVE: *Games for the Brain,*
"answers attached," a book
of puzzles and games.

回家, 一放下
huijia,   yi fangxia

就跑到厨房去
jiu paodao chufang qu

ABOVE: *Story of the Young Chairman Mao,* published by Shanghai Youth and Children Publishing Co. (1958). Mao has come home from school very hungry because he has given his lunch to a poor classmate.

ABOVE: An advertisement for The World's Best — Great King Oil, *"Remedy for headache, toothache, skin eruptions, athlete's foot, colds, nausea, stomachache, and fever."*

Strength & Power

補丸 補針 命保賜他維 長命牌

VITA-SPERMIN
THE WORLD'S GREATEST TONIC

WAH LOONG

TELEPHONE
NO 25931

115 JERVOIS ST.
HONGKONG

TRADE MARK

MADE IN HONGKONG

DIOSCOREA

Wai-Shan-Kwok

Yem Knotty   Used as a beverage to soothe dry membranes

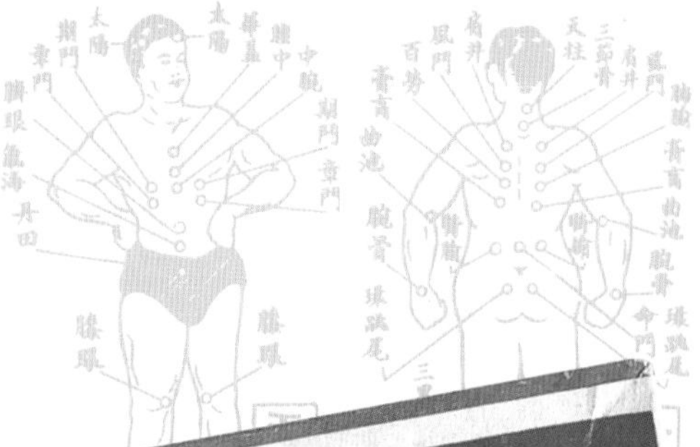

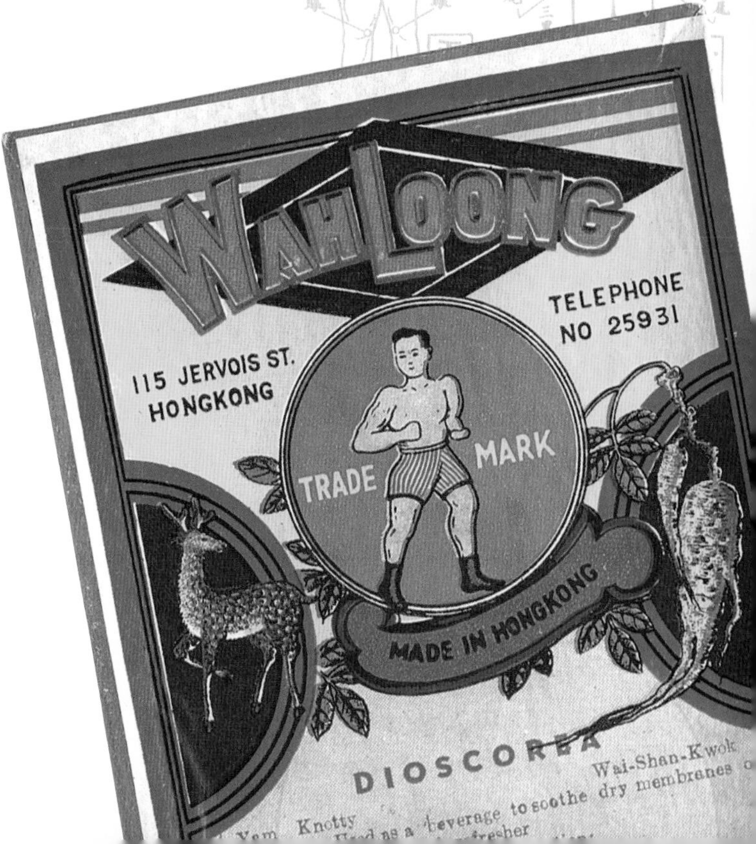

ABOVE: "One Tablet Pill," "One Heart Ointment," and "Pain Killer," from the Yung Sing Pharmaceutical Co.

LEFT AND BELOW: Cigarette packaging art
after the Revolution and into the space age.

BELOW: Cigarette packages celebrating industrialization after the Revolution.

<small>ABOVE:</small> Cigarette packages touting progress, clockwise from top left: "Thousands of Miles," "Satellite," "East Sea," and "Radio Wave."

ABOVE: Hong Kong actress Lin Dai says *"I like Good Look Cigarettes"* on a postcard advertisement.

ABOVE: **A Revolutionary label from an unnamed product promoting** *"Affluence, Peacefulness, and Auspiciousness"* **(1950s).**

RIGHT: **Always facing left, a collection of pins celebrating Mao Zedong.**

RIGHT: **Porcelain figurine of a character in the Revolutionary ballet *Red Army Detachment*.**

These images of the Cultural Revolution were made using the ancient art of papercutting.

ABOVE: Clockwise from top left: Cigarette tin, pack of Alliance Cigarettes, "Farmer's Pleasure" matches, tin of stamp pad ink.

BELOW: *"The Motherland Is Moving Forward"* reads this Revolutionary slogan on a teapot, shown here with a tea tin from the 1960s.

Dancers from *The White-Haired Woman*

traditional story adapted as a Revolutionary ballet.

ABOVE: "Anti-American Matches"
and "May 1st Matches,"
Kuen Ming Match Factory.

LEFT: Chairman Mao — young, old, and
surrounded by the army's ten marshals —
on dishware from the 1960s.

177

ABOVE: **Revolutionary dresser mirrors.**

"Strongly Support Our Farmers," reads this poster promoting Shenyang "East Is Red" farm machinery.

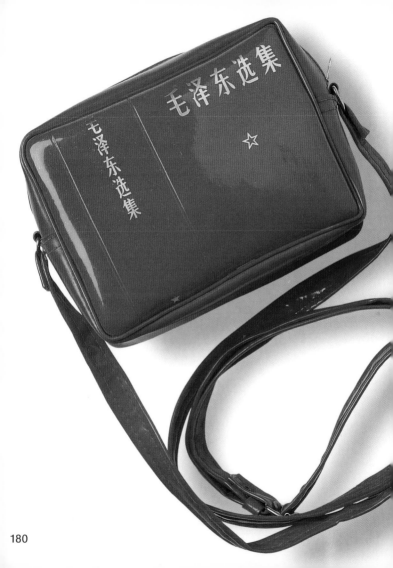

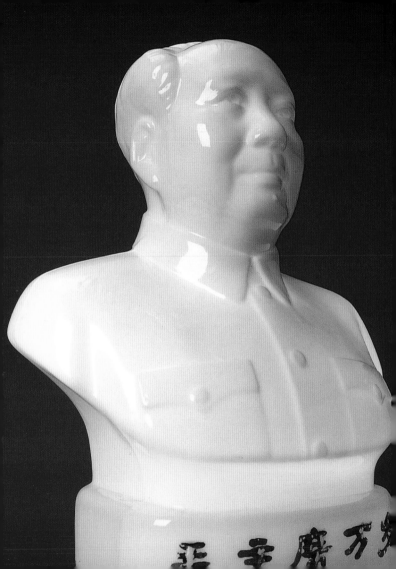

ABOVE: Mao rendered on plastic plaques and pins.

LEFT: The legend on this bust reads
"Long Live Chairman Mao for over 10,000 Years."

ABOVE: Faces of the laborer, the farmer, and the soldier on a poster that reads *"Revolutionary Organization Is Good"* (1967).

標　商

工農牌

"Spring Farming Productivity"

"Strengthen National Security"

"Going to the Countryside"

"Transportation and Industry"

ABOVE: The fervent climate of the Cultural Revolution
is permanently on display in mid-century public
monuments such as this throughout China.

RIGHT: "Rural Portable Theater," a poster painted by Xian Li Liang, which sold in 1966 for .15 Yuan (less than one cent U.S.).

ABOVE: A soldier stands on patrol in the corrupt streets of Shanghai on a playbill for *The Guard and the City Lights*, a play performed by the Wu Han Group Victory Troop of the People's Liberation Army.

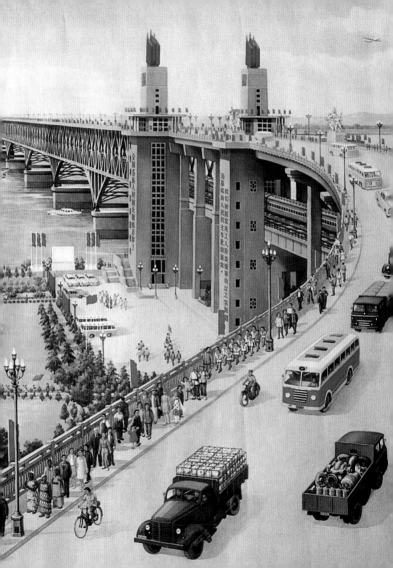

南京长江大桥

南京长江大桥

南京长江大桥

Views of the celebrated
Yangzi River Bridge at
Nanking, a showpiece of
the Cultural Revolution,
on a poster (left) and
matchbox covers (above).

LEFT: **Poster of "Chang Sha Train Station" painted by Chang Yi Ching, Hunan Publishing Co.**

ABOVE: **Scenes of Chungking on matchbook covers.**

"A voyage on the sea needs a pilot. Go far with the ideas of Chairman Mao," reads the slogan on this portable radio.

ABOVE: **The Zhu Jiang radio from Guangzhou, Zhu Jiang Province Radio Factory.**

BELOW: "Service for the
Public" radio and
Dan Guan radio, both
from Shanghai Toy,
14th Factory.

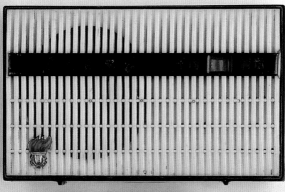

BELOW: The Super Harmonica, *"complete with several melodies."*

200

Vacuum JUG

In the culture of tea, a thermos is never far away, fueling the day for shopkeepers, laborers, office workers, and housewives.

SUNFLOWER
ART. NO. 410
CAPACITY 1.60 LITRE

ABOVE: The red flag reads *"Productivity Competition"* on this advertisement for Industry and Commerce brand batteries.

202

噴殺蟲藥
(消毒養蟲)

日曬
(消毒衣服被褥)

滅鼠
(預防鼠疫)

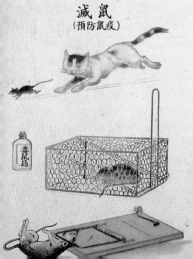

常洗澡換衣
(預防斑疹傷寒和回歸熱)

LEFT: Hygiene tips on a poster for homemakers. Clockwise from top left: *"Killing insects with DDT," "Using the sun to kill germs," "Showering and changing clothing often," "Killing rats."*

ABOVE: Cleaning time in the Buddhist Temple at Longhua.

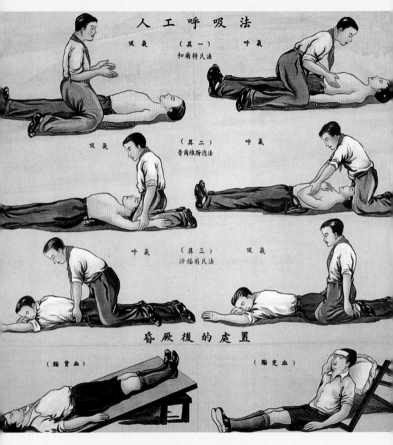

人工呼吸法

吸氣　（其一）　呼氣
扣爾特氏法

吸氣　（其二）　呼氣
普爾維斯德法

呼氣　（其三）　吸氣
沙福爾氏法

昏厥後的處置

（腦貧血）　　　　　　　　　　（腦充血）

ABOVE: Resuscitation techniques, from a poster titled *"Emergency Lifesaving Methods."*

行人过马路要走横道线

九江车辆监理所宣 83·10-1

九江火柴

非机动车让机动车

九江车辆监理所宣 83·10-4

九江火柴

严禁驾驶室超座

九江车辆监理所宣 83·10-7

九江火柴

维护交通秩序，人人有责。

九江车辆监理所宣 83·10-9

九江火柴

严禁扒车，拦车。

九江车辆监理所宣 83·10-6

九江火柴

严禁拖斗载人

九江车辆监理所宣 83·10-10

九江火柴

ABOVE: *"Road Safety Awareness for Drivers,"*
a series of matchbox labels on Jiuo Jiang Matches.

207

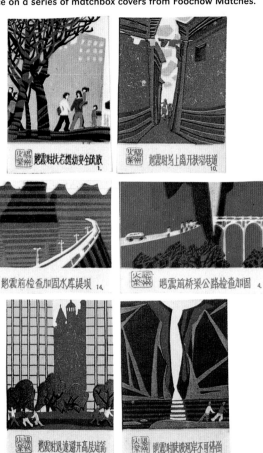

RIGHT: *"Goldfish"* brand mosquito coils, *"Best in the World."*

保血蚊香
MOSQUITO DESTROYER
BEST IN THE WORLD
"FISH"
MOSQUITO DESTROYER
挽回利權
振興國貨
THE BLOOD PROTECTION CO. LTD.
保血有限公司
土製治蚊香塔
MOSQUITO DESTROYER
MADE IN MACAO
本號代售
正牌魚嘜蚊香

ABOVE: **A soft-drink bottle from Asia Soft Drink Factory.**
RIGHT: **A bottle of China "Aerated Water."**

ABOVE: **The Shangnan Three-Speed Electric Fan.**

注册 万里 商标

万里牌

LH 微型

电压　110伏或220伏 交流或直流
周率　50～单相
功率　450 瓦

电吹风
DIAN CHUI FENG

IH型感应式

电压　110伏或220
周率　50～
功率　450瓦

用途：供理发吹风、医学、生物研
　　　究所、化验室、实验室及一般
　　　工业烘焙之用。

上海市日用五金工业公司所属

长发型发鬌

海燕式

风凉式

蝴蝶式

ABOVE: Clockwise from top left: "Long Hair Chignon," "Ocean Swallow," "Butterfly," and "Cool Breeze," from a manual called *Hair Cutting and Styling* (1980).

LEFT: An ad for "10,000 Mile" brand electric hair dryers.

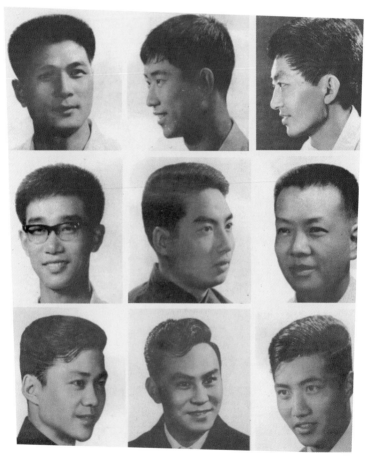

ABOVE: Hairstyles for men from a book by the Shanghai Barber Study and Supply Company (1980).

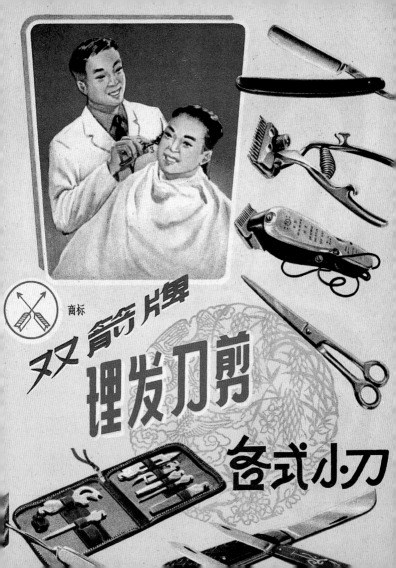

电影故事

DIANYING GUSHI

电影故事

DIAN-YING GUSHI

4
1958

9
1958

Covers of *Dian-Ying Gushi*, the "magazine of movie stories" (1958).

电影故事
DIAN-YING GUSHI

6
1958

电影故事

小芹   二黑

Poster for the movie *Xiao Er Hei Is Getting Married*,

小二黑結婚

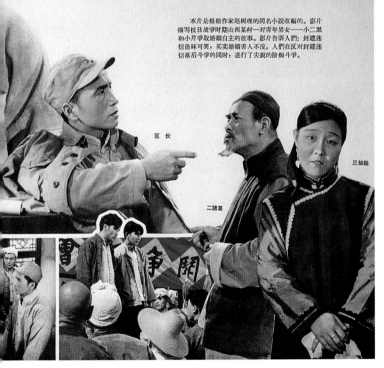

本片是根据作家赵树理的同名小說改編的。影片
描写抗日战爭时期山西某村一对青年男女——小二黑
和小芹争取婚姻自主的故事。影片告訴人們：封建迷
信愚昧可笑，买卖婚姻害人不淺。人們在反对封建迷
信落后斗爭的同时，进行了尖銳的阶极斗爭。

区 长

三仙姑

二諸葛

Beijing Movie Studios (1960s).

ABOVE: *Ten Days in a City Called Dragon,* starring Xu Feng,
The Queen of Action Movies, Federation Pictures.

ABOVE: *The Glamorous Princess Who Moves Commoners,*
starring Wang Fo Yong, Yung Hwa Movie Company.

達豐影業公司第二部出品 全部歌唱狂笑大喜劇

呆佬添丁

少新權　李學優　譚秀珍　何驚凡　紫羅蓮　梁醒波

聯合主演

電影發行部發行

顧文娟　監製

吳回　編導

LEFT: *Mr. Fool is Having a Baby*, starring Leang Sing Po and Chi Lo Lan, from Motion Picture and General Investment Co. Ltd.

ABOVE: Flyer for B movies playing at the Kamwah Theater, Hong Kong (1950s); from top to bottom: *Beauty*, *Private Feeling Between a Boy and a Girl*, *Story of Siu Yuet Pak*.

Movie story magazines from Hong Kong (1950s).

Foggy Hong Kong

Female Playboy

224

Beauty and Disaster

Marriage

225

第五號特派員

時事間諜小說

初集

Inexpensive pulp novels from Hong Kong (1950s).

LEFT: *Detective Stories of the 7th Uncle* "True murder stories from the toughest detective in Canton."

LEFT: *Secret Agent Number 5, Current Spy Stories.*

ABOVE: *Funny Hero, Stirring up the Authorities*

227

ABOVE: *Little Wong*, a comic book
by Yuan Bou-Wan (1949).

Manhua (comics)
from Hong Kong
(1940s –1960s).

TOP: *Tears
of Shattered
Dreams.*
BOTTOM: *The
Infinite Power
of Lord Buddha.*

RIGHT: *Robot Caught the
Vampire at Night.*

鐵甲人

夜提殭屍

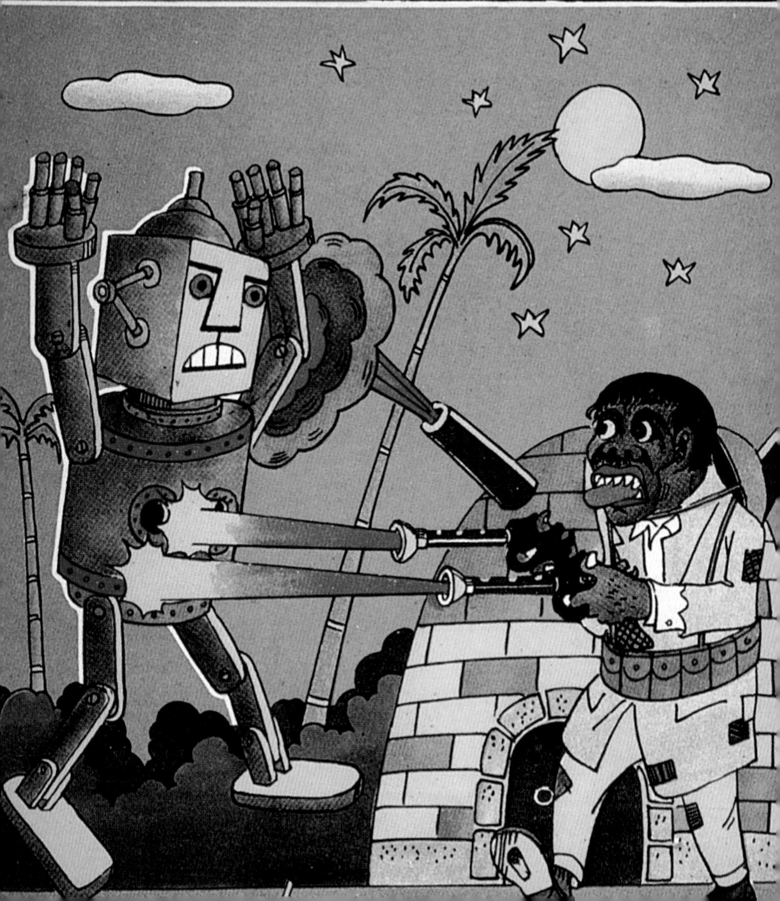

*The Iron
Arm Man*

*Coup
d'État in
the Palace
of the
Thunder
God*

*The
Savage
Planet*

LEFT: *Flying Mouse vs. Flying Hands.*

ABOVE: *Na Cha*, the hero of a famous Chinese creation myth.

ABOVE: *The Red Hand,*
a Robin Hood–style hero.

A collection of LP records from Hong Kong and Taiwan including Crown,

Chong Wha, Ring Ring, Beautiful Sing, Universal, and Tian Sing Records.

ABOVE: *You, the Thief of Hearts*, sung by Lee A. Ping.

RIGHT:
Hit songs
from the
swingers movie
*Red, Green,
Man, Woman*
and a 45 called
*Off Beat
Cha Cha*
by The
Sparklers.

THE SPARKLERS

OFF BEAT Cha Cha

CD-9

香港榮華製片公司出品

紅男綠女
電影插曲

O.K. 伯親家
歡樂菁春

REP-100

ABOVE: Shrink-wrapped statues of the Buddha. RIGHT: Block-print poster of a Buddhist scripture called "The Western Paradise," in the form of a pagoda maze. Both items are from religious supply shops near popular temples.

金剛般若波羅蜜經

LEFT: *"Hail to the 10,000 Armed Quan Yin."* A prayer to the popular goddess of Buddhism, shown here as a porcelain figurine (1970s).

陳聯馨

陳聯馨
MADE IN CHINA

陳聯馨
MADE IN CHINA

馨極品硃

CHINA

CHAN LUN HING
DEALER IN
BEST QUALITY JOSS STICK
MADE IN CHINA

陳聯馨

東

東

粤

陳

東

陳

馨極品硃砂長壽香

品硃

CHAN LUN HING
DEALER IN
BEST QUALITY JOSS STICK
MADE IN CHINA

...SED OF REEDS COVERED WITH
...E MADE FROM THE DUST OF
...OUS WOOD"
...TOBER 5TH. STREET
...ACAO.

LEFT: Old
temple
incense
made from
"odoriferous
wood."

243

RIGHT: A symbolic formal headress made of paper, for burning at funeral ceremonies.

LEFT: Offerings of "Hell Money" are burned at memorial ceremonies to placate home-less spirits. These bills depict former presidents of the United States.

"Joss paper" burned in ceremonies on